FROZEN SOCKS
NEW & SELECTED SHORT POEMS

ALAN PIZZARELLI

HOUSE
OF HAIKU

www.houseofhaiku.com

First Edition
Printed in the United States of America

ISBN # 978-0-9626040-3-4

House of Haiku
Bloomfield, New Jersey

Book Design by Donna Beaver
Cover photograph © by Alan Pizzarelli
Author photograph © by Donna Beaver

For Donna

Contents

INTRODUCTION

Alan Pizzarelli was one of the youngest of the early pioneers of haiku in the United States and one of the brightest. At the Haiku Society of America's meetings in New York City in the early 1970s, he startled the original members of the Haiku Society of America with the innovative and experimental audacity of his new kind of haiku and senryu. The young poet I wrote about in an intro to his *Zenryu and Other Works* 1974 (published in 1975), calling him "the mad cosmic comic . . . crazy with-it monk of Zenryu," has become one of America's haiku masters. Through the years, Pizzarelli has also come to be recognized as one of the most important practitioners and spokespersons for haiku's related genre, senryu. To this day, he continues to shake the haiku world with his groundbreaking poetic styles and dazzling, yet pared down and simple wordcraft.

This latest collection of his holds an amazing variety and range of accomplished and exceptionally outstanding work. From his early poems about amusement parks and carnival acts to his more recent excursions into the worlds of baseball and cowboys, urban landscapes and back-alley glitter, Pizzarelli has managed to open up haiku and senryu to the whole panoply of modern American life. This book gathers it all together in one volume, including work from his first book of haiku and senryu, *Karma Poems* (1974), the marvelous *Flea Circus* of 1989, *City Beat* (1991) and *Senryu Magazine* (2001), up to the *Windswept Corner* of 2005 and beyond.

From his buzzing fly escaping the slaP to his fat lady bending over the tomatoes, from his jeweler closing the folding gate beneath the stars to the gas station man pointing his nozzle to show the way, from the flapping strip of burlap on the young tree to the car coming out of the car wash, Pizzarelli has filled the American haiku and senryu world with imperishable and wonder-filled images that have immeasurably enriched our literature. I would like to take time here to just briefly discuss two of his masterpieces, one a haiku and one a senryu.

First, the senryu. This senryu is a paragon of both simplicity and richness and is one of his most enduring and endearing poems. It's made up of only seven words:

> done
> the shoeshine boy
> snaps his rag

This may not only be one of his best known senryu, it may be the most famous of all American senryu. Allen Ginsberg is shown photographing it in the movie *The Source* when it was featured on a theater marquee on 42nd Street off Times Square in New York City. This special installation of haiku on abandoned theater marquees was part of *The 42nd Street Art Project* that took place in 1994. The poems remained in place for a year or more. This poem is memorable for the way it gives us a vivid example of how human nature can strive to do well and take satisfaction in even the most menial task—how one can take pride in a work of perfection, whether it is a great jazz solo, a perfect curve or a flawless shoeshine. There is, too, a touch of humor in the poem that warms the heart. A universal moment of humanity that in its effect can rival in our imaginations the cinematic images of a Charley Chaplin.

> twilight
> staples rust
> in the telephone pole

Nature's not just birds and flowers, it's also death and decay . . . and rust. The rusting of the staples is nature taking away the freshness, the new shiny glint of the original staples through the passage of time. This is one of Alan's most well-known haiku. As has been pointed out by several critics of American poetry this poem follows in a tradition of haiku established by the Japanese masters in its expression of the feeling of *sabi*, or the loneliness of certain objects that the passing of the years have marked in a special way. The staples take on a coloring that can be compared to the patina acquired by old clay tea bowls or the greenish tint that forms on ancient bronze statues. However, instead of taking revered art objects as his focus, the poet takes as his subject one of modern life's most disposable items, giving it with the rust and the pole and the twilight a kind of paradoxically holy status. It's this turn to the ordinary and neglected that makes this poem something magically new and timeless in the present moment.

I wrote in the third edition of *The Haiku Anthology* that Alan Pizzarelli was one of that book's biggest attractions. And that it was too bad I couldn't hang a circus banner from the cover saying, "Don't Miss the Greatest Haiku Act on Earth!" Since that time, Alan has become so well known around the globe that banners are not necessary to attract a crowd. With his podcast, *Haiku Chronicles*, produced and directed by Al and his wife, Donna Beaver, plus his reputation as the senryu editor for several years on the *Simply Haiku* website, and his other activities from speaking at haiku conferences here and in Canada to his teaching haiku and senryu in as far-from-home places as Switzerland, the name Alan Pizzarelli for many people has become synonymous with the words haiku and senryu. As Allen Ginsberg said many years ago at a poetry reading in New Jersey, "if you want to know about haiku, talk to Alan." And now if you want to know what all the hoopla is about, read this matchless book.

Cor van den Heuvel
Editor of *The Haiku Anthology* and *Baseball Haiku*

FROZEN SOCKS

A SILVER HUBCAP

"Call it *a silver hubcap.*"
— Allen Ginsberg

driving
out of the car wash

clouds move
across the hood

off the car bumper
sunlight flickers
across the trees

work done
the garbage man drives off
in a Cadillac

on the peddler's truck
an emptied scale   swings
in the morning sunlight

a trolley car
       rolls into the tunnel

dragonflies re-alight
on cable wires

halting traffic
    the goose crossing
honks back

a honey bee hovers by the yellow curb

an ice cream truck
turns the corner
into the pouring rain

taxicabs
passing through
an empty wine bottle

car beep
                  birds fly off

      evening

in front
of the drive-in movie screen
the tall pines

a bundle of newspapers
    is tossed out
the moving truck

moonlight shatters
from a dewy hedge

a moving van zooms
    along the backroads
                autumn

nightfall
horse chestnuts hit the parked car

in the rear-view mirror
tombstones

cold wind
at the knotted end of the flagpole rope
a washer   clinks

bitter cold
the car's horn blows
by itself

leaning on the car fender
winter mountains

blizzard
resting on my shovel
awhile

sun brightens
    snow   slides off
        the car bumper

wiping the chrome
blue vapors fade

tiny fish
        swaying
into the current
        shadows rippling
    over a hubcap

in the stream
a shopping cart
fills with leaves

crossing the bridge
car wheels humm
over a metal grating

Vup!
a distant tugboat

Manhattan skyscrapers
the sun sets red
in all the windows

dik-duk dit-duk
a loose manhole cover

a hubcap rolls down the midnight street

into its distant sound

smoke rings blow from the giant lips on the billboard

on the bright marquee
a man's shadow changes the letters

in the building's shade
a man winds up
the barking dogs

eyeing the pretty girl
the vendor man inflates a long balloon

the rubberband man
stretches in-between
his sidewalk acts

done
the shoeshine boy
snaps his rag

raindrops plick
on the parking meter
morning twilight

rain wet streets
cars k'plosh & splawsh
the neon puddles

a bright awning is cranked
over the corner fruitstand

in front of the go-go bar
 a broken umbrella
   shakes with the wind

"clean-up" flyers
 litter the street

on the jackhammer
the road worker's belly
ripples

through a hole
at the construction site
a striped cement truck turns

twelve o'clock whistle blows
the painter lowers his brush

McSORLEY'S OLD ALE HOUSE

in the small tavern
the urinals are huge

JUNKIE

on a rooftop
he waits
        shivering

the sky darkens
rain drizzles
the pusher arrives

heating the horse
        sweat oozes
            sniffles

shooting up
he nods out
                cold

now
only the sound
of rain

~

slicing a ripe pomegranate
watching the horror movie

the windowpane reflects
a tv cartoon
snow falling

in the tv store
on all the screens
cloned sheep

turning off the tv
sunlight fills the empty room

in the shade
of the animal hospital
white azaleas wilting

shaving the man's head
the barber's short story

the smudge of a kid's nose
    slowly fades
on the bakery window

sun up
cobblestones

blistering heat
  the snow cone vendor
    pushes his cart uphill

on the curbstone
a dog licks the boy's
scabby knees

the brim-shadow
of the fat man's straw hat
lowers over a long sandwich

summer moon
everyone sitting
out on the stoops

the wrecking ball hangs in the air
beside the abandoned house

b owling

a few snowflakes
fall on the candy store window
the lights go out

in the empty concert hall
the sound of radiator pipes

darkness moves
over the rooftops

snow light

blue shadows loom
the snow corniced street

sun breaks
ice falls from the pussy willows

above the antique shop
an old metal sign
squeaks in the cool breeze

snow piles up
the barber shop pole
spins into itself

twilight
staples rust
in the telephone pole

AMUSEMENT PARK

just before dawn
a beach ball   floats
across the stillness of the pool

lightens

under the boardwalk
sunlight brightens and fades

the tattoo'd man
walks onto the crowded beach

lying in the sun
she unties her bikini top
and falls asleep

rolls over

"drool inwardly!"
she mutters to her husband
on the crowded beach

a monarch flutters out to sea

drop of ocean
in my navel
reflects

the amusement park

the setting sun
lights the top
of the high striker

in the shadows of the trees
by the amusement park
        a firefly

on the boardwalk
high above the crowd
a man on stilts

spinning cotton candy
the girl with the teased-up hair

the jelly judge
refuses another taste
of the prize-winning jam

by the spinning teacups
the operator waxes
his handlebar mustache

at the seafood stand
the skinny kid orders
another dozen mussels

the old sailor's
bathing beauty tattoo
wrinkled too

high tide
the awning lifts in the wind

on the merry-go-round
that empty blue bench

from the ring toss
at the far end of the midway
the barker's hoarse voice

at the turtle race
the boy finishes
his ice cream cone

before the fireworks
    fireflies

the teenage boy falls in love in the barrel of fun

the taffy pullers
      the taffy pullers
the taffy pullers

winning a budgie
at the spinning wheel
            it flies from the cage

above the arcade
a yellow moon flashes
through drifting clouds

skee ball
the kid with a fistful of tickets
wins a plastic bubble pipe

PORNO MOVIE

the girl
        loosens her bra
starts peeling off panties
        darkens

25¢

in the fun house
blow holes lift the girl's dress

a drunk walks straight through the crooked room

across the steeplechase
iron horses race
into the glittering night

selling helium balloons
a man with a high-pitched voice

the fortune teller
snaps the curtain shut

sudden thunder
the boardwalk
blacks out

under the boardwalk
bullet shells glint
below the shooting gallery

the lifeguard's chair
leaned on its back

snowflakes fall
on the dismantled
kiddie rides

the ferris wheel turning
into the fog

THE FLEA CIRCUS

carried from the car
the ventriloquist's dummy
looks around

the magician
farts
no smell !

still skeptical
of the hypnotist,
he walks off on all fours

backstage at the theater
ordering everyone around
the puppeteer

squinting
to read the sign
"optician"

scraping his shoe
against the curb
the passing parade

later found out
the gypsy fortune teller
knew me

drifting into sunlight
a milkweed seed
meets a sparrow

light rain
on the young tree
a strip of burlap   flaps

Indian summer
the acupuncturist brings his cactus
back outside

the bronze statue of a man
in a long coat and fedora
suddenly steps off the pedestal

Halloween –
the gothic teenager
doesn't wonder what to wear

long after the party
a helium balloon
slowly turns in mid-air

holding
the little girl's doll
it pees on my pants

the visiting mother-in-law
re-arranges the furniture

the dog runs after the stick
i pretend to throw

the bearded lady
hangs her wash
against the wind

misplacing her glasses
the hoarder
finds another pair

late in the evening
a midget hoses the sunflowers

scarecrow
coughs
butterflies

waterbug running by the froGULP

buzzZ
　　　slaP
buzzZ

the fat lady
bends over the tomatoes
a full moon

reaching for
    the wind-up toy
        it rides off the table

across the tightrope goes the star of the flea circus in a pink tutu

BASEBALL POEMS

at the produce stand
a kid with a baseball
plays catch with the awning

BASEBALL HERO OF VACANT LOT

tossing a stone
up into the air
    Cak
       clouds

       Crash
    dropping the stick
whistling down the street

~

billowing clouds
drift from puddle to puddle
on the baseball diamond

in the clubhouse
the catcher on a hitting streak
slips on the same old socks

the great soprano sings
the national anthem
from second base

leaning for the sign
the pitcher rotates the ball
behind his back

struck out —
    back in the dugout
        he kicks the water cooler

at the edge of the dugout steps
the manager shakes some dirt
in his hand

at shortstop
between innings
sparrows dust-bathing

mid-mezzanine
   i eat
a hand-me-down hotdog

bases loaded —
at the crack of the bat
the crowd pops up

7th inning stretch
the facade's shadow reaches
the pitcher's mound

the score keeper
peeks out of the scoreboard
spring rain

october rain
the tarpaulin ripples
across the infield

saturday afternoon
as the ballgame ends
geese return to the outfield

leaving the game
the click of his cleats
fade into the clubhouse

game over
all the empty seats
turn blue

THE WINDSWEPT CORNER

on the windswept corner
traces of a puddle
fade

morning twilight
a truck driver gently
unloads sacks of clams

from the corner newsstand
an old man's old dog
carries home the paper

a billowing cloud
resumes its shadow
across the twin towers

march wind
girls in slacks turn the corner
of the flatiron building

above broadway
a swinging piece of siding   exposes
an ornamental cornice

on a high scaffold
painters brush
the dentils white

the barber napping
teeters on the back legs of a chair
toupée askew

a butterfly alights
on the brownstone's rosette

down a windy side street
slanted chimneys

outside the church
a gum-stuck sidewalk

through the open door
of the barber shop
a milkweed seed   drifts

among the crocuses
a black top hat
where the snowman stood

on the window ledge
above the candy store
a nest of wrappers

on the theater marquee
the word "c mplete"

in the boutique window
 a mannequin
     suddenly *moves*

in the antique shop
the rumble of a passing train
k'plinks's a dusty music box

as boxes roll down
    the cellar wheel chute
        old hands reach into the light

sudden rain reeled in on the wash line the doll's clothes

left outside
in the hailstorm
a pogo stick

thunder
gulls fly from the rounded roof
of the bowling alley

below the dripping eaves
puddle ringlets widen
in a radio flyer

in the dark garage
sun beams through the holes
of a hanging pail

mid-day heat
a thin man walks in the narrow shade
of the supermarket

behind the police station
robins chase
the tiny moths

a crooked footpath
    cuts through the vacant lot
to the corner liquor store

in a fallen crow's nest
along the fairway
a golf ball

fading across the grooves
of a glacial rock
    a bird's wet footprints

hottest day of the year
a breeze in the distant treetops

it's here!

in the early moonlight
a mockingbird does
a crow   a gull   a cricket

summer twilight
leaning against the redbrick factory
feeling the day's heat

leaves scatter
behind the gun store

down a side street
            snow
under the striped sawhorses

a snowdrift slides off
   the pitched roof
      dripping sunlight

christmas morning
the cats claim
the unwrapped boxes

a strand of tinsel
falls on the toy tracks   sparks

sixties christmas dinner
the long table lined with cakes

starry night
the jeweler closes
the folding gate

on the windswept corner
stamping the snow
off my boots

THE RISING MIST

a screen door slams
deer leap into the rising mist

a loose kite
         dives
in the summer mountains

   wind sparkles up stream
  an old oak
creaks

      sunset
      into the sound
      of crickets

a butterfly alights in her hair
wings unfold   summer mountains

macro clouds drift
beyond the backyard fence

cut down
the tree that leaned against the house
leaves its shadow

a piece of buttered popcorn
floats in the garden pond
swirling colors

the totem carver
hoses down the large pole —
scent of cedar shavings

a raven flies off
pine needles scatter
into a drift of snow

a leaf
        falls
into the still lake
        rippling
the wilderness

with each gust of wind
the leaves of the silver maple
lighten

the wild turkey
   turns its gold-tipped tail feathers
into the morning sun

on the old oak
one branch of leaves   turned red

in the still silence
    the slow fall
        of cottonwood seeds

in the rotted hollow
        of a tree stump the ghost orchid
            reappears

the old cottonwood's roots
slant the bluestone sidewalk

chasing the woodpecker
off the bird feeder
the chickadee   s
                h
                i
                t
                s

in the knotted oak
the deep imprint
of a chain-link fence

a leaf
sticks to it
bitter night

planting a garden
the sky nightens

cucumber vines
climb the scarecrow's legs
it begins to rain

right after saying
i was never stung by a bee
guess what?!

withered garden –
never thought
i would miss the bees

blossom storm
swirling into
falling snow

flinging the Frisbee
skips off the ground
curving up   hits a tree

petals

sunrise
an old woman
picking mushrooms

sundown
each firefly
has its own blink

all along the path
of the nature reserve
poison ivy

hot night
whirring cricket wings

the cricket cage door
left open   starry night

meteor

the cloud fades back
into blackness

Wearing her
"World's Best Mom" T-shirt,
she wallops the whining kid.

sunrise
in the quaint little village
the cry of a lunatic

as he stokes the fire
smoke
from our guest's toupée

listening
to the politician's speech
I eat a baloney sandwich

first spring day in the
retail store
the smell of new appliances

The cross-eyed customer
tells the salesman:
"I'll take them!"

at customer service
the incessant complaints
of a parrot

At the brassier factory,
the busty receptionist
says "Can we help you?"

meeting an old acquaintance
in the freezing cold —
same old chatter

in the supermarket
the spinster smiles
at the cucumbers

in the dairy aisle
a bald man
inspects the eggs

telling a joke
the butcher splitting ribs

after i wax
the kitchen floor
the dog runs in place

happy to see me
the dog lifts his leg

at the animal hospital
a dog-eared copy
of a pet care book

at the community hall
one old lady shouts "BINGO"
the others say "shit"

in the nest
of the pet rock
pebbles

in the schoolyard
one of the saplings
has failed to bloom

Asking the little girl
if the tooth fairy came:
"yeth," she says.

burying a dead bird
the small boy
hums the wedding march

on the road
a possum
not playing possum

a cow
jumps over the fence
utter destruction

grazing sheep
gossip
about the new farmhand

the feminist
reads her speech
dressed like a man

PMS
i eat the roses
i brought her

"I'm serious!"
he shouts
wearing a pinwheel hat

"He's a lousy lover"
she tells the girl
who has eyes for me.

on a date
the actress
still acting

at the drive-in movie
i undo her bra
double feature

eating the burnt meatloaf
he forces a smile
at his beautiful wife

all excuses spent
i tell my wife
about my alien abduction

after the divorce
she fits back into
her old dress

the surgeon
orders his steak
well done

"They're not all the same"
says the gynecologist
eating oysters.

telling us a joke
we laugh
at how un-funny it is

the critic
reads another book
he doesn't like

by the sagging fence
of the nursing home
old ladies

old married couple
the husband threatens suicide
        the wife tastes the soup

a loud fart
"what did you say?"
she asks

at Walden Pond
  i eat
    a granola bar

tip-toeing near
the sleeping bear
i snap a twig

in the dark woods
    the glowing eyes of bigfoot
      ends the weenie roast

slipping on a sheet of ice the sky

a UFO
whatever it was
i need a change of underwear

walking past
the brain trees in Central Park
i recall a dream

every other time
the interrogator slaps my face
i admire the plum blossoms

"Just trim the hairs
in my nose & ears!"
Says the elderly man –
"How short?"
Asks the barber.

"When you're dead, your dead!"
i say —
a sad silence
falls among the guests
"tennis anyone?"

another day
in the universe…
what's for dinner?

PARODIES

The turnip-puller
Points the way
  With a turnip.

~ Kobayashi Issa

the gas station man
  points the way
with a gas nozzle

~ *Pizzarelli*

Visiting the graves,
the old dog
    leads the way.

~ Kobayashi Issa

the town drunk
lets the butterfly
    lead the way

~ *Pizzarelli*

I cough and am still alone

~ Ozaki Hosai

I fart and am not alone

~ *Pizzarelli*

A huge ant
Walks over the tatami:
The heat!

~ Shiro

A giant lobster
Walks over the tatami:
Wearing a bib!

~ *Pizzarelli*

At a grass hut I eat smartweed,
I'm that kind of firefly

~ Takarai Kikaku

With the morning-glories I eat my meal,
I'm that kind of man

~ Matsuo Basho

At the festival I wink at the ladies,
I'm that kind of firefly

~ *Pizzarelli*

Write me down
As one who loved poetry,
And persimmons.

~ Masaoka Shiki

Write me down
As one who loved senryu,
And loose women.

~ *Pizzarelli*

séance
a white
moth

~ Raymond Roseliep

séance
a white
lie

~ *Pizzarelli*

Trying to forget him
stabbing
the potatoes.

~ Alexis Rotella

Trying to forget her
grabbing
the melons.

~ *Pizzarelli*

i eat alone
& pass the salt
for myself

~ Michael McClintock

eating lunch
with the mime
i pretend to pass the salt

~ *Pizzarelli*

a single tulip!
hopelessly,
i passed on

~ Michael McClintock

a single tomato!
hopelessly,
i keep watering

~ *Pizzarelli*

a stick goes over the falls at sunset

~ Cor van den Heuvel

a stool pigeon goes over the falls at sunset

~ *Pizzarelli*

a wheelchair
rolls
in from the waves

~ Cor van den Heuvel

a toupée
rolls
in from the waves

~ *Pizzarelli*

Lily:
out of the water...
out of itself.

~ Nicholas Virgilio

Lily:
out of the water...
out of her suit.

~ *Pizzarelli*

TANKA BLUES
& other poems

a passing cloud
darkens the tavern window
still thinking of her
i lift my beer mug
the coaster sticks to it

troubled…
i gaze
at a slender maple
with its branches snow-bent
in spring

snow blows off
the paper birches
nobody cares

clipping gray hairs
in my mustache
  white narcissus
     droops
by the garden pond

painting windows
i dream
of better things to do
still
painting windows

night arrives
all the guests
have gone home
even the crickets are silent
under the Pleiades

in the attic chest
a puzzle's piece of sky
falls from an old love letter

rain drums
on the car roof
missing her
i turn the radio on
then off

after hearing
the prognosis
rain
falls harder
outside the hospital window

sparrows are building nests
with the poems
i shredded

the flowers
i bought her wilting
and me with this illness

trying to hide
her grief
she chops the onions

with a broken umbrella
in the pouring rain
that kind of day

at the race track
losing tickets
folded into tiny sailboats

all summer long
looked for the bald eagle
later
stopt looking
saw two

summer's almost gone
  a yellow leaf
  clings to a long strand
    of spider silk
  twirling in mid-air

  today i saw
my first nuthatch
        heading
          down the tree bark
  like some nuthatches do

gray november day
i sneeze
and hundreds of starlings
fly out
the bare trees

at the traffic light
a man holding a plunger
gets into a taxi
the light turns green
they drive off towards a toilet

with no money
    i go
    snow viewing

bored
in my lonely room
a naked woman
walked in
and that took care of that!

lying naked
we tell each other the stories
behind our scars

after love-making
the sound of rain
        returns

woke up this mornin'
my kid's pet snails
                stuck
on the kitchen ceiling
went back to bed

opening the mailbox
nothing but a screak

poisoning the pigeons
the old lady
late for church

i'm sitting here
watching an old western
all of the actors are dead
they are ghosts
riding out of tombstone

only the distance peaks
between the horse's ears

riding
down the highway
a pickup truck
loaded with wooden indians
passes through a hawk's shadow

tonite i gazed
into the universe of infinite star galaxies
and thought
"how insignificant i am"
still, i washed behind my ears

sitting on a park bench
solitary musing
gusts of wind
scatter the leaves
— not a cloud

i wait calmly
in a boat unmoored
the night sky
a reminder
of my empty heart

at the nursing home
old folks sit
saying nothing —
outside the window
a dry creek

closing the casket
a wisp of blond hair
                    flies out

    visiting her grave
snow falls
    on the white carnations
in time
    even the stars'll be gone

snow flurries
in the graveyard   bells

a wrapped gift
on the child's grave
winter rain

a gloomy day
washing dishes
a cricket
jumps right down
the drain

all dressed up
with no place to go
went anyway

taking the day off
idly seeking
the elusive woodpecker

woke this morning
    cradled in the upper branches of a tree
no more wine for me

on the bluestone sidewalk
a kid's chalk drawing of the sun
brightens this cold gray day

this warm february day
is only a tease —
mother nature lifting her skirt
above her knees

well worn ruts
   well worn ruts
     over here over there
     they drive me nuts
   well worn ruts
well worn ruts

in the mirror store
a japanese woman sits
head in hand
head in hand
head in hand

up all night arguing
the rising sun
turns the mountains red

separated
from wife & kids
now
only this ringing
silence

after reading
my son a bedtime story
i go home

exhausted
i flop on the bed
it too collapses

walking past the legless beggar
my own blues
soon forgotten

eating pomegranates
fingers stained red & wrinkled
deep autumn

in the honey jar left open
mice drowned

read a book on zen
THAT THICK
learned nothing

ZEN CATHOLIC

asking the zen master
"what is the sound of
one hand clapping"

no use turning
the other cheek

A KOAN

Make a sound with no movement

ZEN REPLY

the sound of one hand clapping
is not as loud

SITTING MEDITATION #1

think of nothing
& not even that

the mountain
doesn't care
what I think

on a cool damp morning
the priest rubs his velvet cape
and zaps the altar boy

always thought
that when i retired
i'd write more poetry --
now here i am growing a garden
it's the same thing

tonite
nothing to write

but this

a spark
falls to the ground
        darkens

that's it

all day
cutting off
          fishheads
knowing nothing

          lasts

in the graveyard
a mourning cloak flutters
over the incense ashes

octopus
in the dark wash basin
new moon

HAIKU RAILROAD BLUES

bending back
along the railroad track
                    tiger lilies

as the train passes
   the heads of geese
      pop out of the tall grass

snow falls from trees
         rumble
of passing boxcars

far down the railroad tracks
   the brakeman's lantern
      gets lost among the fireflies

a train horn
   fades into the distance
boxcar wheels

THE WINDOW SHADE

a gentle breeze
        fills the drawn window shade

a narrow line of sunlight
    w i d e n s
                across the floor

    dust brightens
the shade snaps shuT

the shade springs open
frozen socks on the line

ACKNOWLEDGMENTS

Frozen Socks is a collection of new and selected haiku, senryu, tanka, kyoka, parodies, and other short poems written from 1969 to 2015.

The author is grateful to the editors of the following books and periodicals where some of these poems first appeared:

Haiku Magazine, Modern Haiku, Brussels Sprout, Mirrors, Haiku Canada Newsletter, Haiku Society of America Minutes, The Village Voice, Mainichi Daily News (Japan), *Inkstone* (Canada), *Haiku Highlights, Cicada* (Canada), *Tweed* (Australia), *Seer Ox, Dragonfly, Bottle Rockets Press, An Anthology of Haiku by People in the United States & Canada* (Japan Airlines), *The Haiku Canada Anthology* 1989, *Frogpond, High/Coo, Raw Nervz, Byways Press* (England), *Acorn, Prune Juice, Tundra, Simply Haiku, Street Lights – Poetry of Urban Life in Modern Tanka*, ed. Michael McClintock & Denis M. Garrison, *Baseball Haiku*, edited by Cor van den Heuvel & Nanae Tamura (W.W. Norton & Company, 2007), *The Haiku Anthology* edited by Cor van den Heuvel (Doubleday, 1974; Simon & Schuster, 1986; W.W. Norton, 1999), *Haiku North America Anthologies* (Press Here), in addition to the following limited edition chapbooks by the author: *Karma Pomes* (Raw Egg Publications,1974), *Zenryu & Other Works* (From Here Press, 1974), *A Silver Hubcap* (Pizzazz Publications, 1976), *Hike* (Pizzazz Publications, 1984), *Baseball Poems* (Broadside, 1988), *The Flea Circus* (islet books, 1989), *Amusement Park* (islet books, 1990), *City Beat* (islet books, 1991), *It's Here!* (islet books, 1995), *Senryu Magazine – Out to Lunch* (River Willow, 2001), *The Windswept Corner* (bottle rockets press, 2005), *The Canary Funeral* (House of Haiku, 2012).

Sheet music for the poem, "the ice cream truck" (pg. 5) composed by Thomas Terreri.

Translations of Japanese poems by R.H. Blyth and Hiroaki Sato.

Special thanks to Louis and Alan Ginsberg, Harold G. Henderson, Cor van den Heuvel, Anita Virgil, William J. Higginson, Michael McClintock, Tadashi Shokan Kondo, Alexis Rotella, and Nick Virgilio. Also, to all the poets and artists who have crossed my path over the many years who encouraged and inspired me along the way.

Made in the USA
San Bernardino, CA
11 December 2016